From
"I wish you'd....stop"
to "I am glad YOU..."

CREATIVE COMPASSION

CREATIVE COMPASSION
A Handbook for Spiritual Growth
by Blake Steele
Copyright © 2003 Scandinavia Publishing House
Drejervej 11-21, DK 2400 Copenhagen NV, Denmark
Tel.: (45) 35310330   Fax: (45) 35310334   E-Mail: jvo@scanpublishing.dk
Text copyright © 2003 Blake Steele
Photo copyright © 2003 Blake Steele
Design by Ben Alex

Printed in Singapore
ISBN 87 7247 266 9

All rights reserved. No part of this book may be reproduced or utilized in any form or by any means, electronic or mechanical, including photocopying, recording, or by any information storage and retrieval system, without permission in writing from the publisher.

SPIRITUAL VISION SERIES
by Blake Steele

A God to Desire
Being Loved
Radical Forgiveness
Creative Compassion

SPIRITUAL VISION SERIES

CREATIVE COMPASSION

A HANDBOOK FOR SPIRITUAL GROWTH

WORDS AND PHOTOGRAPHY
BY BLAKE STEELE

scandinavia

This book series is specifically designed to inspire and guide you towards spiritual healing and transformation. Through a unique blend of words and images, scriptures, poems and exercises, it gives you tools to take spiritual reality from a mental understanding to a heart experience where all the good things happen.

Creative Compassion focuses on God's compassion and creativity, and our call to become our most genuine selves, freely expressing His Love and beauty in the world.

It is my heartfelt wish that God will use this little book to inspire your own unique gifts and dreams towards their complete fulfillment in Him.

BLAKE STEELE

I, THE LORD, AM THE MAKER OF ALL THINGS... Is 44:24

God is the source of existence. All power comes from His infinite being. He is the lush cornucopia of Creation. He dreamt up the stars, the galaxies, the planets, and created them by the power of His will. He has made a universe that is ingenious, mysterious, teeming with Life and astonishingly beautiful.

If you want to see what God loves, look around: sun and moon, seas and rivers, clouds, rain and snow. He built the mountains and fills the fields with flowers. His Spirit gives existence to animals, birds, fish and insects... and every human being: the old and young, the strong and weak. All Creation is the artistry of the supreme Artist; the manifest dream of creative genius.

Become compassionate, just as your
Father is compassionate. Luke 6:36

And Jesus revealed that the Source of all is compassionate Love. This is very good news, for compassion is the highest expression of Love. It is unconditional in its nature and pure in its intent. Compassion is a constant outflow of goodness without secondary motives or a hidden agenda. It is a free movement of God as infinite blessedness pouring out healing, happiness and harmony in the same way as the sun radiates light and heat from its fiery core.

We think space is empty:
it is full of God singing,
laughing and dancing
two steps ahead of the speed of light.

10

The Lord is loving towards all He has made. PSALM 145:13

11

12

AND THE GLORY YOU HAVE GIVEN ME I
HAVE GIVEN TO THEM; THAT THEY MAY
BE ONE, JUST AS WE ARE ONE. JOHN 17:22

Jesus expressed God's compassion in His consuming passion to free us into union with God. It was His intention, His clear purpose, that compassionate Love would make us one in God's glory—the harmonious beauty of Love.

Only compassion can unify humanity, for it is the warm, welcome embrace of limitless Love loving our entire self—every shamed, rejected and ridiculed part of us—and flowing through us to embrace others with its inherent kindness and care.

> IF ANYONE SEES HIS BROTHER
> IN NEED AND CLOSES HIS HEART
> AGAINST HIM, HOW DOES THE LOVE
> OF GOD LIVE IN HIM? I JOHN 3:17

The Earth has enough resources to meet every genuine human need. All humanity needs to be happy is a widespread compassionate perspective of life. When at last God's compassion becomes the one law of life, ruling freely in every heart, human suffering will shrink to a tiny fraction of its present immensity, for people will truly love to bless and care for each another.

God wants to flow through your entire being:
trickling, bubbling, streaming in a human/divine mix:
making you infectious with His blessings of Love.

17

18

COMPASSION IS OUR TRUE LIFE

I AM THE VINE, YOU ARE
THE BRANCHES... JOHN 15:5

In this saying, Jesus reveals who we are in relation to Him. We are like branches on one vine. We come out of Him. Each of us is a unique expression of His infinite Life. Compassion is born through a realization of who God is, and who we are in Him.

...YOUR LIFE IS HIDDEN
WITH CHRIST IN GOD. COL 3:3

Christ is wise and good, innocent and blameless, tender and strong, remaining in the integrity of His own being. He is fully free in His fearless Love and complete truthfulness. Nothing can delude or defile Him. And He is our true life: deeper than every wound and falsehood that denies Him.

If Christ were not free He could not love you

WE ARE PURE SPIRIT

> FOR WHO KNOWS THE THOUGHTS OF A
> MAN BUT THE SPIRIT OF THE MAN,
> WHICH IS IN HIM? I COR 2:11

In our deepest essence, each of us is a spirit, a living presence in His presence; light in His Light: silent, watching, a witness of Him and us. From the perspective of pure being, we are not our thoughts or emotions. These things pass through us and we experience them. But we are not what we experience, rather the hidden one who experiences.

(Christ experiences our thoughts + feelings)

It is essential to fully wake up to this fact. Only then will we understand that our real life actually is hidden with Christ in God—and so, our most essential and true being is nothing less than pure compassion. Therefore, to surrender to His compassion is to live from our deepest self, and to unite soul and body with eternal spirit—the only wholeness possible.

— our true nature.

one surrenders to Him + to one's deepest self

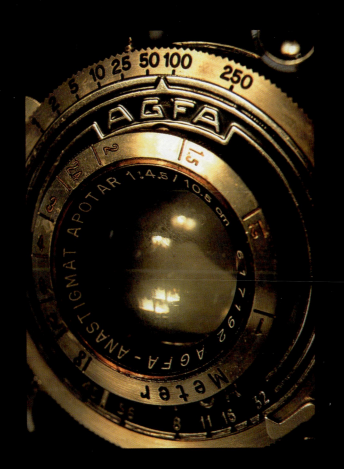

*In the moment of time,
without expectations,
this is my happiness,
this my completion:
I open my heart
and out comes Your singing.
Simple and open,
the movement is fluid,
a river that flows
from a motionless sea.
I am quiet and watching
from eternity.*

AND WE ARE A SOUL

our soul

Our soul is the mysterious child of the union of pure spirit with pure biology. It is the traveler, journeying through life, ever curious and hungry for experience. Created by God, it yearns to know the living God and the wonders of the world. It is able to hold within it countless contradictions and is the womb of both the old self and the new. It encompasses within us all that is wounded and needy—and is capable of becoming a radiant, living mirror of Christ.

It is the soul that bridges the worlds of Spirit and matter. It flows with thoughts and feelings and is capable of wild and inventive imaginations. It receives, it ruminates; it acts and responds. It is designed to co-create with God. Our soul is like a living, growing tapestry of all we have experienced, of all we dream. It is wondrous and bewildering, beyond our conceptions—but if we live in Love it grows as God intends it to grow and gives birth to His purpose.

Love is the soil
our soul's need to live + grow in.

WE HAVE AN "OLD SELF"

...LAY ASIDE THE OLD SELF WITH ITS PRACTICES... COL 3:9

Hidden in every one of us is a painful grief of wounded innocence that is the source of a sense of self that feels separate from God, and thus always goes astray.

This self is insecure and afraid. It nurtures a grasping neediness and an anxious fear of loss. This separate self's inner dynamic of grief, insatiable need and fear creates a system of faulty beliefs, self judgments, crippling emotions and defense mechanisms in our mind and body. It is these things that combine to create a perception of life that blinds and binds us. This is the old self that Christ came to free us from.

Apart from Him we are a closed door; a shivering gazelle hiding in a bush; clinched fists grasping for wind; busyness with too little meaning,

30

...HE IS NOT FAR FROM EACH ONE OF US, FOR IN HIM WE LIVE AND MOVE AND HAVE OUR BEING... Acts 17:27-28

Happily, just beyond the blinded perception of our old self is an infinite ocean of Love from which springs the fountain of Life, the pure, healing compassion in which we live and move and exist. How beautiful beyond words it is to wake up and experience that underneath all human sensations is the boundless Being of ecstatic fullness we have called God and Love.

We can only experience God through who we are.
Apart from Him we cannot relate to such clarity and openness,
such freshness and freedom, such vulnerable tenderness
or innocent intimacy. This is our alienation.

The New Self

> ...AND PUT ON THE NEW SELF WHO IS BEING RENEWED TO A TRUE KNOWLEDGE ACCORDING TO THE IMAGE OF THE ONE WHO CREATED IT. Col 3:10

The new self is God's image growing in the ground of our soul. It is the divine fruit of grace and the soul's faith. This self is awake and grows through knowing it is united with Christ and limitlessly loved.

It is the new self that loves God completely and becomes strong by the work of Christ to free us from the crippling influences of the old self. It is the new self that throws its heart wide open to celebrate the Love that it gladly allows. This is the child of Life who is inspired to birth newness, to let Love's eternal freshness flow through all the mystery and wonder of its radiant being out into the world.

SALVATION MEANS LIBERATION

> ...WORK OUT YOUR SALVATION... FOR IT IS GOD WHO WORKS IN YOU TO WILL AND TO ACT ACCORDING TO HIS GOOD PURPOSE. PHIL 2:12-13

We are saved by grace. The Hebrew word for saved means to be opened wide and made free. In the Greek it implies to be delivered, protected, healed and made whole. We are opened, and made whole and free by unearnable grace as God works in us to will and act in harmony with His good purpose.

It is a fact. The old self cannot liberate us no matter how hard it tries, for the old self's very nature is an anxious sense of separate existence. How can a sense of alienation from God ever bring us into union with God? It will always function according to its own nature of insecurity, possessiveness and fear. Its perpetual instinct to try to fix and preserve itself will be the motivation for everything it initiates. God's purpose is to liberate us from the old self and form the new self within.

Why do we keep giving God away?
He who is our strength and beauty.
Why do we keep on bartering away our God?
He who is our freedom.
Blind need—born of that first betrayal
of our vulnerable innocence.
It is need that with greedy, grasping hands
drags us away from that quiet,
brimming well
of flowing, flaming love
that heals us.

37

ONLY COMPASSION MAKES US BLOSSOM AND BLOOM

Only God's compassionate Love can open and free us, for He loves without conditions or limitations and with no other agenda than to heal us for the sake of Love. Deep inside, our center must ✓ shift from <u>self-need</u> to <u>His fountain of Love</u>. It is the word of truth flowing to us in the freedom of grace that illuminates our minds and softens our hearts, forgiving and freeing us to remain in His Love. This centering in Him is experiential liberation.

→ *from Self-supply to His supply.*

Practicing openness to God's river flowing,
to holy breath breathing,
to Love's flame burning,
to Christ's light shining.
Practicing openness to God.

Compassionate Love opens everyone's heart. This is stronger than a good argument.

the giver + the receiver

> MAY HE GRANT YOU YOUR HEART'S DESIRE,
> AND FULFILL ALL YOUR PURPOSE. Ps 20:4

It is only by following Love that we come to realize that our true God-given desire is for freedom to grow in the limitless blessings of Love, and that our truest purpose can only be revealed in Love's freedom.

You are in this world to grow a self that express the Light and beauty of Christ through the entirety of your being. There has never been a soul like you and never will be again. Your one-of-a-kind soul holds unique patterns and desires. If you resist the urge to discover and fulfill your deepest heart's desires you will resist the unique expression of life and Love that God wants to create in you, and a treasure will be lost that cannot be regained in time.

42

43

> ...THAT YOU, BEING ROOTED AND GROUNDED IN LOVE, MAY GRASP... HOW WIDE AND LONG AND HIGH AND DEEP IS THE LOVE OF CHRIST WHICH SURPASSES KNOWLEDGE... EPH 3:17-19

Follow Love. Trust Love. Don't hold anything back. Open your whole being to the Ocean of Love in which we exist. Discover how your deep, true needs and yearnings come from God and lead you home to happiness. Make a firm commitment that you will trust God's call to freedom. Find the beauty you love—and do it! Become your most authentic self.

Wisdom plays within the boundaries of the holy,
solely a child at heart and free—as God is free—
in wise spontaneity: To dream, to believe,
to become through deeds,
to be a maker of Love's beauty.

46

...OUR OLD SELF WAS CRUCIFIED WITH HIM... Rom 6:6

It is when we choose to allow God to bless us without limits that our old self's resistance is most clearly revealed. This is normal. It is the fearful nature of the old self that perverts and blocks our growth in Love—it always has and it always will. That's the nature of its game.

If we try to fight the old self by ourselves, then we are trapped in it. But by relating to it in an entirely new way we can shift the dynamics of the old self's game. In Christ we actually are free to step out of it. This comes when we are finally willing to shift our identity. In Christ, my old self is dead. This means I am not the insecure, needy or fearful thoughts and feelings that pass through me. I am not the aching sense of isolation I have experienced. I am not the self I thought I was: unaware of God and fighting for control. My identity with all this is finished. I am someone else—someone who is loved without limit.

IF ANY MAN IS IN CHRIST, HE IS A NEW CREATION... II COR 5:17

I am in Christ. My life is pure spirit hidden in Him; my soul is perfectly designed to grow in His Love and birth His new creation. His arms are opened wide to me. And so, because my true self is united with Him, I open my arms wide to welcome everything within me. All is forgiven; all is welcomed home to the feast of His Love. Welcome home wounded old self. Welcome beloved spirit and soul. Welcome good body and all my marvelous senses. I open my heart and welcome His Love to bless everything!

God loves my body
and makes my soul sing peace.
His light flowing into me opens my being.
I slowly unfold in Love.
In the mingling of spirit and sense,
heaven kisses earth and earth heaven.
This is a feast!

Go out to the streets... and bring in the poor and crippled and blind and lame. Luke 14:21

All that we hold back from His circle of Love will remain outside in the loveless dark of the old self, working to bind and blind us. For the sake of all that is beautiful and good, let God love you. Allow it! Say yes to His great Yes of you, every part of you—especially all you avoid, detest and resist. Bring it all in! Let His Love greet all, forgive everything, and bless, bless, bless.

Meet your most painful past experiences fully, naked of all judgments. Forgive yourself of the interpretations you have imposed. Don't run from your own Life!

Experience fully embraced is the treasure of the soul.
The treasure chest opens.
Out springs compassionate wisdom!

> BECAUSE THY LOVINGKINDNESS IS GOOD, DELIVER ME; FOR I AM
> AFFLICTED.. AND MY HEART IS WOUNDED WITHIN ME. Ps 109:21,22

No matter how painful your life has been your experience holds valuable lessons that become yours only as you embrace them fully. Rejecting our experience is rejecting our life and creates within us a terrible sense of separation and loss. Our soul has been designed by God to embrace life and to grow wise by fully having its life-experience, the good and bad, the beautiful and the ugly. Letting Love reunite you to painful past experience is the essence of forgiveness and courageous trust in God.

Embrace your experience fully with complete forgiveness until all rejection melts away. *Yes I feel you pain.* I embrace my experience. I am completely forgiven and forgive everything. *Thank you Lord for the hidden treasure of this experience.* Miraculously, through this unconditional acceptance of Love, an inner sense of trauma dissolves. Compassion is the only meaning that remains—and with it, true wisdom.

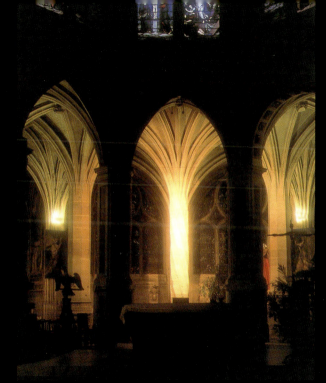

Do you not know that you are the
temple of God, and that the Spirit
of God dwells in you? I Cor 3:16

Your body is God's house. It is not designed to be a storehouse of repressed pain and negative emotions. Let God wash you until your body sings with His Life. This is the saving power of Christ made real!

Each experience we reject distances us from our own soul and from God, from our body and from Life. Each aversion we reclaim brings us home to Him—like a bird landing in a cherry tree full of ripe cherries—every experience full of the juice of Life, embraced, ingested, making us more fully alive! Let His river flow into every corner of your soul. Let Him deepen your passion to live! Reclaim all of your body and God will laugh in you like a silver stream, clear and bright, singing in the miracle of His Life.

What Is This Miracle Called Life?

IN HIM WAS LIFE; AND THE LIFE WAS THE LIGHT OF MEN. JOHN 1:4

Jesus came to give us fullness of life in union with God. Growing in life is His purpose. But what is life? Life is a miracle of awareness in Him. It is the light within our brains and bodies. It is spirit in matter. Life is not a concept; it is a creative growing happening; a miraculous movement of change; an awakening we must surrender to in order to fully know. It is a wonder that fully blossoms in Love.

And what is Love but the power that makes life grow good and strong and free. It is the nurturing impulse, the desire for all things to become beautiful and all people to overflow with happiness. It is harmony. It is joyous union.

In Christ, life and Love are completely one. His Love wakes us up to the value and wonder of life: and life makes Love creative, innovative, bursting with beauty.

*Come on then, and laugh
and let God through,
this Holy One
who waits to be freely expressed
through His creatures.
Surrender to the gift
you are given,
the one that links
you to the new creation
of love and beauty
that God wants to become in you.*

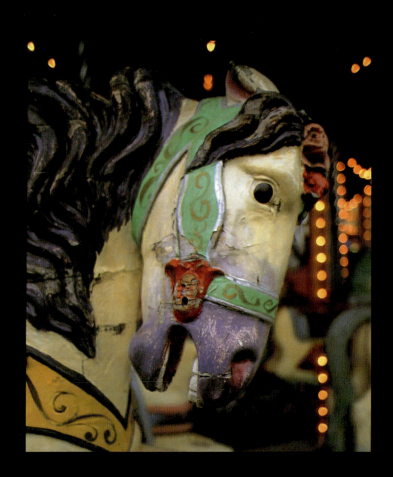

For in Him all things were created... Col 3:16

Life in Christ is purely creative. Through Him all things have been made. He is the wisdom of God giving form to the entire Universe. It is He who is holding all things together: every molecule; every cell. He is astonishingly innovative and vibrantly alive!

God is the infinite wellspring of blessing, pouring out gifts, giving and brimming, bestowing and blessing, and loving to bless in the rivers of blessing.

Then I was beside Him, as a master workman...playing always before Him, playing in the world... Prov 8:30-31

His creative wisdom is playful and free and always at work. It is in this wisdom that we are free to be playful in a creative partnership with God that births new creation.

> FOR THE KINGDOM OF GOD DOES NOT
> CONSIST IN WORDS, BUT IN POWER. I COR 4:20

The root of the word power, in New Testament Greek, means the ability to manifest the possible. Jesus demonstrated faith as creatively manifesting the possibilities of God in Love.

> ...WITH GOD ALL THINGS ARE POSSIBLE. MATT 19:26

Creativity is a state of open receptivity to God's creative potential waiting to happen. A creative mind makes new connections, sees new possibilities, and envisions the invisible becoming visible. Creativity is the birth of newness. It manifests. It bubbles and boils over. It is what happens when we are awake and aware and robustly alive.

 The kingdom of God is manifesting what is possible in Love.

64

GOD SAID, "LET US MAKE MAN IN OUR IMAGE..." GEN 1:26

You may believe that you are not a creative person. But being made in God's image every one of us is constantly creating. With every thought, word, emotion and action, by the beliefs that form your perceptions, you are creating your own unique expression of life.

What are you busily creating? Is it a life full of Love, beautiful dreams, new opportunities, surprises and celebrations, balance, and blessing? Or is it expressions of the old self you still believe you are? Are you helping to create a status quo that resists God's reality and destroys His Creation, or are you expressing His compassionate presence? We cannot escape our destiny. We all create expressions. Why not discover what you really love in your deepest heart and in partnership with God create expressions of that? Why not share the beauty of His Love with your world?

God's Glory

God's glory is revealed in all He creates. The Universe clearly shows the immense breadth of His imagination and ingenuity for it is bursting with energy and brimming with the living music of existence. God is the fountain of existence, super-alive and wildly creative. He celebrates Life with splashes of color and infinite intricacies of form.

Out of His Spirit come inspirations of creative expression: for God is robust with Life, loving the story, the drama, the fiery dance of Love—the adventure of it all! It is His great Spirit that loves to celebrate in our celebrations, dance in our dances and sing in our songs. All this zeal and zest, wisdom and creative wildness is nothing but glory!

GIVE UNTO THE LORD THE GLORY OF HIS NAME... Ps 29:2

The whole Universe is constantly singing God's name: tree songs, stone songs, fire, wind, earth and water singing; the sun silently shouting—God! But the song of freedom and fairness, of compassion and new creation is waiting for mankind to wake up and sing. We are called to give to the Lord our expressions of His name.

It is when we fully surrender through Love to the fountain of His Life that new creation spontaneously breaks out! It is our new-creation self that passionately loves life and is born singing. And its song is ecstasy. It is joy! It is the free working of God's creative potential expressing the glory of His Love!

*The Creator of all is the highest beauty of Love,
wondrously desirable—sublimely delicious.
It is the beauty of God that causes the ecstasy of angels.
His glory spangles the galaxies
and is hidden in the microscopic,
right down to the radiant roots of matter.*

*It is from there, out of the source of all things,
that the tender glory of God's Love
pours into our innermost being
to illuminate our heart and fulfill our most primal longings
to be understood, accepted, valued and cherished.
And it is from there, out of His eternal fountain of Love,
that the urge comes to discover and fulfill
our highest destiny.*

ALL THAT MATTERS IN CHRIST IS
A NEW CREATION. Gal 6:15

God has promised that one day there will be a new heaven
and earth. And yet, new creation is always happening—right now!
It is Love's creative expression; it is human fruitfulness that is
juicy—it is the essence of God creatively revealed. And this essence
of God's heart is compassion.

GOD MAKES ALL THINGS BEAUTIFUL IN HIS TIME. Ecc. 3:11

It is through the union of creativity and compassion that Christ
births a new creation of celebrative people through whom
compassion flows to heal and creativity acts to make the world
beautiful with Love.

> AND LET THE BEAUTY OF THE LORD
> OUR GOD BE UPON US... Ps 90:17

Allow the Love and beauty of God to be upon you. Slow down. Take time to be aware. Look up and feel starlight. Listen to the wind and water. Sense growing things. Nourish your God-given delight in life and the beauty of Creation. Ponder the living words of grace that open you to the Living God. Fall into His Love for you and fall in Love—for only Love opens you to the glory of existence.

And the more we open to His glory the more singing and dancing, poetry and paintings, new songs and celebrations will break out, creating atmospheres of awe and wonder, freshness and freedom, playfulness and confidence which inspires minds to open, hearts to soften, souls to expand and sets the spirit free.

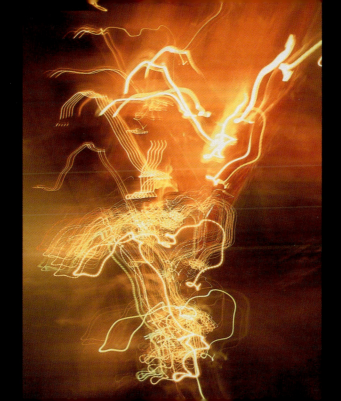

For what goodness and beauty
will be theirs! Zech 9:17

Why not fill your home with goodness and beauty? It doesn't take money, only care and awareness. And why not fill your church, your business, your community with the beauty Love inspires? This entire Universe is a gift. It is a wild expression of God's self-giving. God loves to give gifts: and the bigger the gifts the better. Doesn't it make sense that the Creator's children should be wildly expressive of Love and beauty?

We can senselessly give away flowers. We can write little notes of appreciation. We can honor others and seek Christ's hidden beauty in them. Let God inspire you. Spread the freshness. Share the wonder. Start from where you are. Be the shining child of God you are!

> LET THE LITTLE CHILDREN COME UNTO ME... FOR THE
> KINGDOM OF GOD BELONGS TO SUCH AS THESE. LUKE 18:16

We all know how much children need love. But children also need beauty. Spend time with them in nature. Explore with them the wonders of God's creation so their souls become deeply connected to life. Let them soak up the whirr and buzz, swish and splash of it through their senses. Help them understand that in God Love and wonder and beauty are one.

We have all been created for God's glory and are drawn to it like bees to pollen. It is in an atmosphere of awe, alive with Love and life and creative beauty, that children of all ages fall in love with God and the miracle of everything. It is His Spirit that makes our eyes shine, our hearts laugh and our bodies dance. Let's be honest, if our expression of God does not captivate the hearts of our children and awaken the hidden child in us, then the wonder of His glory must be missing.

**Shout to God with
a ringing cry.** Ps 47:1

*Sing it, shout it, dance it, spin in it,
write it, speak it, think it, share it,
paint it, sculpt it, put it in your cooking,
in your business, in your home,
in the way you relate to all things:
this Love that urges us on,
this glory that captivates the heart
once the heart's eyes open to see
the wonder of a Universe
wholly open to God,
limitless with possibilities,
radiant with beauty.*

PERSONAL VISION

YOU DID NOT CHOOSE ME, BUT I CHOSE YOU, AND APPOINTED YOU, THAT YOU SHOULD BEAR MUCH FRUIT... JOHN 15:16

Personal vision is Christ's call for you to bear much fruit in the world. This vision comes from God through your deep heart as the fullest expression of your unique self in Christ. It is a creative response to the urge of Love within you to bless the world and the need of the world to be blessed. It is born out of a growing passion for the beauty of God to be known and the good of humanity.

Our deepest purpose can only be realized in confident trust. Fear will always block it, for our deepest purpose is to fearlessly express His Love in the world. The passion to birth new expressions of God's Love and beauty comes right out of the Life of God and the new self that our old self always resists.

> THEN YOU SHALL SEE, AND YOUR HEART SHALL BE GLAD,
> AND YOUR BONES SHALL FLOURISH LIKE THE NEW GRASS... Is 66:14

Do you want to discover your deepest purpose? Get in touch with your own soul. Map it out on paper. What do you most deeply love? Write it down. What do you value above all things? Write it down. What connects you to God in your heart? Write it down. What human needs deeply concern you? Write it down. What gives you a sense of joy and freedom? Be utterly clear. Trust God. Trust Love. Open up and let your heart's desires be revealed.

You will know His call because it will feel completely genuine to your soul and will impel you to grow in Love. Fulfilling personal vision is an audacious act of creative faith working through your surrender to let God Love you completely. It is a journey into spiritual maturity and your greatest fulfillment.

Fear always wants to make Love feel guilty for being so free.

88

Be opening! Dance your soul awake!
Love the opening words
which create an opening spirit.
Be Loved... and, sing it!
When we become infectious with joyous Life,
when we become so tenderhearted we ache,
we are just beginning to realize
what it is to become disciples
of the Great God our Maker—
He who is a lush, overflowing abundance
of liberating Love.

Behold, I do a new thing. ...Will you be aware of it? Is 43:19

Personal vision is a freely made choice. You needn't discover it to be saved. Christ has saved us by grace. But if something in you wants to know His greatest goodness and beauty, then no matter what, follow His Love; experience the way of spiritual transformation; allow God to surprise you with His creative freedom. He will carry you to your truest heart's desires, to personal vision, and into the full power of His quiet revolution of Love.

*Let your love be tamed by wisdom—
then make it wild with beauty!*

94

APPENDIX

A PERSONAL TESTIMONY

In the early 1990's I felt Jesus was asking me to find a way to express the poetic vision I had been writing about for years. God opened the doors and with a small group of dedicated followers of Christ I developed a foundation called United Compassionate Artists' Project. Our intent was to bring God's compassion through the arts to suffering people and find innovative ways to share His Love with our community.

Over the next six years we gave close to fifty musical concerts for the poor and over 100 free concerts of poetry and music for the community. We also regularly visited several nursing homes for the elderly: singing, visiting them in their rooms, bringing a touch of God's sunshine into their lives.

During this same period, our local hospital asked us to develop a music program. Through this we gave intimate serenades of love to over 6,000 patients and their family members. Traveling from room to room with guitar, voices and Celtic harps, we came with only one intent: to open our hearts wide to God's Love and let Him freely happen. Time and time again the hospital rooms were filled with the wonder of His presence.

These patients and their families became my teachers. They transformed my life through their love, tender vulnerability and courage as they faced broken bodies, heart attacks, cancer, strokes—and even death itself.

I will close with a few poetic memoirs which I hope give you a taste of how beautiful fulfilling personal vision became for me.

Encountering Heaven

We entered the room, a harpist, the singer and I. Masseuses were there, loosing joy with a dance of soothing fingers. We sang spiritual songs. The masseuses sang along. The woman in the hospital bed just had to sing too, (the music being too beautiful to resist). People gathered in the hall. They had come to the song like bees to flowing honey for the harmony was gorgeous. The masseuses kept up their happy work, absorbed in the movement of the music. We all knew—everyone felt it—heaven was flooding the room. God was the harmony we were voicing; the instruments in our hands had become Love like the masseuses fingers. Then we sang Amazing Grace, harp, harmonica and many voices chiming it.

A lady from the next room stood in the hall, eagerly waiting for us to come into her husband's room. We came, aglow with the blessings of Love. The man's head glistened with metal sutures; an unfeeling arm hung listless at his side. His face spoke bewilderment and sorrow. He felt the holy presence with us even before we started to sing and asked for our prayers—after all, we had just stood in Heaven and remained in the flow of it. We harped, sang, and prayed.
He wept.

An old friend of his had also died that day... Spiritual grace is like a sweet, invisible balm. We are privileged to pour it into the wounds of each other's souls so they might heal. We, christened by love, troubadours of the Holy, left his room, noting that the lines upon both their faces said, joy, and hope, and that their eyes were shining.

We saw them a week later. He was considerably better in every way: still stroke stricken, but stronger, clearer. She grasped my hand, looked directly into my eyes and said, "When you came and sang, that was the turning point for him, you know."

99

WILD COMPASSION ENTERS A NURSING HOME

Shake out your wild hair, woman of the holy winds,
and bear your bread, your flashing bouquet of flowers,
to the lonely, decrepit woman who spits on her shoes,
from whose mouth spittle runs in slow streams.
Dance with your wild tambourines
to the creaking sounds of wheelchairs
rolling down vinyl-tiled, long, empty, halls...

There is a man who cannot talk, strapped in a big chair.
He stares, noticing the glint of Love's fire in your eyes
as you pass by, and sighing, remembers young words.
It's been a long time since he's had a kiss.
You touch his hand. A smile crosses his crusted lips.

SOME SAY THAT MUSIC HEALS, WHEN MUSIC IS PRAYER

This is a true story. We met him in the hospital elevator. He saw the music in our hands and asked us to be sure and not pass by room 515. We went singing down the halls from room to room, spending another night learning to let the Love flow, until we came to a closed door: room 515. We remembered the man and his quiet admonition and so entered.

Have you ever felt the hush of crises? A crackling quiet filled the room. It may have been the sight of a Celtic harp, or the spirit of Love upon us that made us welcome there. She seemed suspended in pain, as if her body was lying on a bed of broken glass. Her nurse was busy doing technical compassion. It seemed a time for silence, or a music that was softer than tears. Ardy wove some beauty upon her harp strings. Amy and I sang gentle love.

With that done, we passed on to the next room. Love met us there too and I would have almost forgotten the woman in room 515 but her husband stood in the hall, shyly seeking to catch my eye. The feeling he sent was clear, she was asking for us to come to her again.

We finished our song and walked back down the hall as a nurse emerged from the room. I asked her what was wrong, thinking such pain was usually seen only in intensive care. It seemed the woman's body was not as near death as was her will. She was soul-weary from too long a fight.

We entered again and the woman whispered across some vast distances, asking us for more beauty. We started a vigil of praise, worshiping the Great Love who began filling the room with a slow-growing wonder. Song after song flowed out as we sang adoration into the heart of healing: adoration quietly flooding out from the full power of a Light we could not see. Like warm, clear water, beauty flowed over her. She calmed and basked in it. Her electric anguish melted away and the woman gazed out upon us with God's eyes. There were birds in the Light of the room.

As we quietly prepared to leave, I, by the instincts of Love, put my hand on her head and prayed for the Holy One to create a miracle—starting in her innermost heart. She said, "That is where a secret working has already begun." The birds went on singing as we moved out into the night.

I returned two days later, curious to know what a small seed of a miracle might have grown into. Room 515 was closed. I knocked and was called in. There was a party going on!

Sitting upon her bed—as noble as all souls should be—sat a vibrant woman surrounded by her children. A daughter from Alaska was taping wild finger paintings upon the walls. A son from California greeted me as I stepped over to look closer at a woman brimming with her own being.

I said, "It looks like a miracle has burst out upon the world here."

Many happy voices chimed out, "Yes!"

I left the room and its visual music behind, silently shouting, "Thank you, thank you, thank you!" as I walked along the ceiling down the hall.

A GOOD DEATH

He was more like a lamb than an old dying man:
his spirit was that tender. He was blind—
but I sensed he could see us. We sang an old hymn,
and he, his frail voice barely audible in the room,
thundered his praises into worlds above us.
We spoke of his coming death.
"I'll be at the wedding feast soon," he said.
We laughed—and knew it was true.
"And you'll be young again," I said, as I touched his hand.
"Yes, and I shall have new eyes..."
he said, his face softly glowing.
We left, each of us savoring our taste of the honey of his peace,
knowing this man was in good hands,
and would die with no bitterness.

So Then, Where Is Our Lord?

Some say that God died or has gone away...
Only those who have died or gone away themselves
could say such things, for God is doing
a trillion deeds of kindness every day.
I've met Him at the bedside of a brave man
whose fingers and toes were dead-black as coal;
I've felt His hands rest upon the hair of a woman
who has battled long with cancer
and who wept to remember His love within a quiet song.
I've sensed Him, with tears on His cheeks,
deep within the eyes of an old woman
who could not speak her anguish at feeling
with trembling hands the cold face of death.
And I've seen Him shine from the faces of a free people
who have been fortunate enough to die for Love
and can now sing it.

Every child of the Creator has the right to dream wildly and to think the thoughts and do the deeds that birth newness in the world. Let your passion for Life grow! Be joyfully wasteful for Love. Give yourself to do the beauty He reveals!

For it is God's own beauty that will save the world.

Choose Life
Birth New Life!

Because you have a New Name
you can get a New Picture
New direction } *by choosing to live*
New beginning } *out of your New name.*

Blake Steele is one of God's vagabonds on earth, traveling to do creative work and share God's abundant love through personal encounters and workshops. A versatile artist, he has written over 2,000 poems, a novel, children's stories, is a lyricist for choral pieces and a photographer. In this book series, he shares his vision, wisdom and awe for God through photography and poetic writing.
www.beingloved.net

power + love - 62

playful wisdom - 61

opened wide + made free - 35